FABULOUS FEMALES, VOL. 2

GRAYSCALE COLORING BOOK FOR ADULTS

Featuring artwork by Ellerslie

Majestic **COLORING**

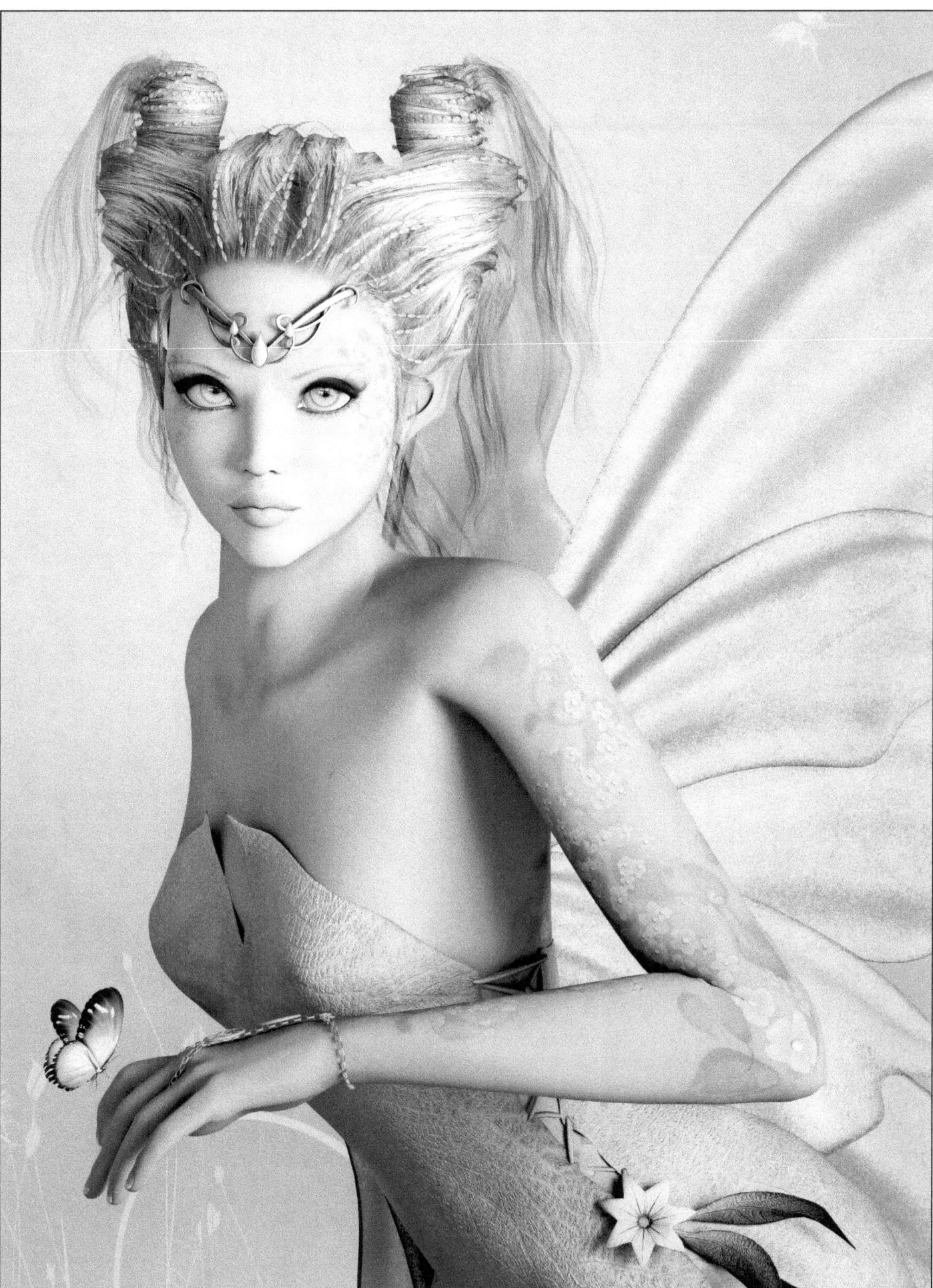

FREE DOWNLOAD

12 FUN DESIGNS FOR YOUR COLORING ENJOYMENT!

This 'n That Coloring Book for Grown-Ups is bundled up in one convenient PDF file to download and print at your leisure.

Sign up for our Majestic Coloring mailing list and get a free copy of **This 'n That Coloring Book for Grown-Ups**.

Click here to get started
http://majesticcoloring.com/thisnthat-free